THREE TALES

by
Margaret Ryan

THE
BIG SISTER'S
TALE

My little brother, Benjamin, is a pest. A big pest. The biggest pest ever. He practises being a pest every day. Even while he's asleep.

Some nights, when he's snoring his head off, I sneak into his room to play with his toys. If he has a smile on his face, I know he's planning something.

Something <u>horrible</u>.

Something <u>terrible</u>.

Something that will really annoy

ME!

I think little brothers should be banned. Big sisters should all get puppies instead. I've always wanted a puppy, one with long floppy ears and sad eyes. Instead, I've got a pest of a little brother. It's not fair.

3

Do you know what the pest did last week, just because I wouldn't let him have my very best shoe box for his snail race? He hid Bobby Bear in the freezer.

Bobby Bear's my favourite cuddly toy, and I was really upset when I couldn't find him. I looked for him everywhere; in the toy cupboard, under the settee, in the garden. Mum helped me search.

"Where did you last see him?" asked Mum.

"In my bed," I said.

We unmade the bed, shook out the duvet, and had a good look. We found a missing sock, an empty jam pot, but no Bobby Bear.

"Benjamin appeared, wide-eyed, at the bedroom door.

You yelled?

"Bobby Bear's lost," said Mum. "Have you seen him?"

Benjamin closed his eyes. "Not recently. Maybe he's been bear-napped."

"Oh no," I sobbed, and cried my eyes out till tea time.

That was when Mum found Bobby. She'd gone to the freezer to get out my favourite fish fingers for tea, and there was poor Bobby, in beside the frozen peas.

"Who put Bobby in there?" asked Mum, looking straight at Benjamin. "Was it you?"

"Yes," said Mum.
And he had.

"I did it for Bobby's own good," Benjamin said. "He's a POLAR bear. He shouldn't live in a bedroom. He should live where it's cold and icy. I was only putting him in his proper place."

"Monster," I cried. "I'll put *you* in your proper place." And I bopped Benjamin on the nose with poor frozen Bobby.

"WAAAAA," Benjamin yelled, and his nose bled on to Mum's new carpet.

Mum wasn't too pleased.
In fact, she was really quite cross.
Mad as a snake, actually. She
gave me a real row. You know
the kind ...

GIRL OF YOUR AGE
OLD ENOUGH TO KNOW BETTER
LEARN TO CONTROL YOUR TEMPER
DON'T HIT SMALLER CHILDREN ETC.
ETC. ETC.

"But Benjamin's a pest," I yelled. "He
gets off with everything, just because he's
younger. It's not fair."

And it wasn't fair either that he got a lollipop, and I got sent to bed early.

And that's another thing. Because he's younger, he's supposed to go to bed earlier than me. He doesn't.

He goes *upstairs* earlier.

He gets into the *bath* earlier, but he stays in there playing pirates till he's as wrinkled as a crinkle chip.

By the time I run my bath, there's no hot water left, and all the bath towels are lying in a soggy heap on the bathroom floor.

The other night was the last straw.

I poked my nose round the bathroom door. "Hurry up, prune face," I started to say when a bubble floated past and went POP on my nose. I gasped.

Billions of bubbles floated all round the bathroom, and Benjamin was standing by the open window popping them and trying to shoo them outside.

"Go on, little bubbles, scoot. If Miranda sees you SHE'LL go POP as well, and that could be very messy. EEEEUCH."

"You horrible little toad, you used up all my new bubble bath."

"I only meant to use a little, to froth up the water for the pirates, but the bottle sort of slipped ..."

"I bet that's a fat lie. I bet you did it on purpose." And I picked up a wet towel, and gave him a good slap.

"WAAAA," Benjamin yelled, as he slipped on the wet floor, and fell and bumped his bottom.

Mum came running. She wasn't too pleased. In fact, she was quite cross. Mad as a snake, actually. She gave me a real row. You know the kind ...

GIRL OF YOUR AGE
OLD ENOUGH TO KNOW BETTER
LEARN TO CONTROL YOUR TEMPER
DON'T HIT SMALLER CHILDREN
ETC. ETC. ETC.

I'd heard it all before.

"Benjamin's a pest," I yelled. "He gets off with everything just because he's younger. It's not fair."

DON'T HIT SMALLER CHILDREN
DON'T YELL AT OLDER PEOPLE

Then I got sent to bed early for yelling at Mum.

I'm fed up with rows.

But I got my own back. Late that night when Benjamin was fast asleep, I tiptoed into his room, and hid his special blanket.

It's an old blue blanket he's had since he was born. He used to drag it everywhere with him, and leave a blue woolly snail trail over the carpet.

Now he just takes it to bed. He hates the blanket to be washed. He likes it smelly and horrible, just like himself. He pulls little fluff balls off the blanket, and stuffs them up his nose. I think little brothers are totally disgusting.

For a moment, though, while he was asleep, Benji looked so nice that I nearly didn't take his blanket. I tidied up his toys to make up for it.

He was really upset about the blanket the next day, so I gave in and gave it back to him.

I suppose I'm stuck with my little brother, but I really would like a puppy. When Christmas comes, I'm going to ask for one.

THE
LITTLE BROTHER'S
TALE

Would any of you like a big sister? You can
have mine if you like.

    For nothing.

        For free.

           <u>Forever</u>.

Do you know what my big sister did last week, just because I *accidentally* told Mum she'd been dipping her fingers in the jam again?

She flushed my dinosaur stickers down the loo. Off they went, whirling round and round. They disappeared down round the bend before I could catch them.

Goodbye, Tyrannosaurus, Brontosaurus, Stegosaurus. I hope you can swim.

It had taken me ages to collect them, too. I'd had to munch through millions of cornflakes, and I only had Triceratops left to get.

James Martin, in my class, was going to swap me one of his Triceratops for the horrible green hat Miranda had knitted me last Christmas.

She's been learning how to knit in school.

Knit one, purl one, drop six...

James said he wanted the hat to keep his guy's head warm on bonfire night.

"Poor guy," I said. "Bad enough being stuck up on the bonfire without having to wear Miranda's hat as well."

I yelled at Miranda that by flushing away my stickers she had spoiled my swap. She went and told tales to Mum. I got a real row. You know the kind ...

YOUR SISTER KNITTED YOU THAT HAT SPECIALLY. IT TOOK HER AGES IT'S NOT NICE TO GIVE IT AWAY THE HAT IS NOT HORRIBLE ETC. ETC. ETC.

The hat *is* horrible, but I had to say sorry to Miranda anyway.

At first I said:

I'm sorry you knitted me a horrible hat, Miranda.

But Mum heard, and poked me.

"Say 'sorry Miranda' properly."

"Sorry Miranda, properly."

BENJAMIN!

"Sorry Miranda," I finally had to say, but I kept my fingers crossed behind my back to show I didn't really mean it.

Miranda sniffed and said, "I accept your apology."

Big deal.

Miranda gets away with everything just because she's older. It's not fair.

It wasn't fair either that Mum said I had to wear the horrible green hat when the weather was cold. She made me wear it one Saturday morning when we were out shopping. I dodged in and out of doorways hoping I wouldn't meet anyone I knew.

No chance. I met everyone in my class.

I'll never live it down.

I think big sisters should be banned.
Little brothers should all get puppies instead.
I've always wanted a puppy. I'd like one with
a spotty coat and a waggy tail. But instead of
that I've got big bossy boots Miranda.
It's not fair.

Another thing that's not fair is bedtime. Miranda gets to stay up later than me, just because she's older.

I try to stay up as late as I can, and stay awake as long as I can, because, when I'm asleep, Miranda sneaks in and plays with my toys.

And she doesn't just PLAY with them, she HIDES them. I have a special place for everything, and Miranda muddles everything up.

Do you know where she hid my cars? In my garage. How stupid can she be? I had the cars all lined up beside my bed for an early morning stock car race, and she hid them away in the garage.

And my soldiers, I had them lined up beside a pile of shoe boxes for a special mountain climb. It had taken me ages to arrange it all. And what did Miranda do? She took back her shoe boxes, and put the soldiers back into their fort.

She never understands. Just like that
time in the bathroom. Her silly old bubble
bath really did slip out of my hand. I was
trying to put everything right when she
came in and made a fuss.

I decided to get my own back. I sneaked into her room while she was out shopping with Mum one day, and played snow storms with her talcum powder – she's got boxes and boxes of talcum powder. She thinks it's so grown up. Soppy sausage.

The talcum powder made a great snow storm. I threw it up in the air, and it covered the bed and all the furniture, and let me make great footprints on the carpet. Trouble was, when Mum came back she somehow guessed the footprints were mine.

Mum always shouts my proper name when she's cross.

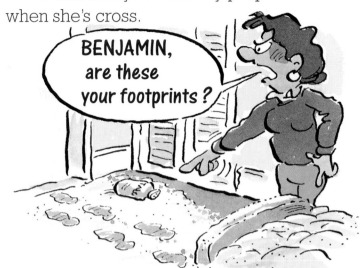

"They might be, or they might be the footprints of the dreaded snow monster."

"You're the only monster here," yelled Miranda, "and that was my very best talcum powder." She made a dive at me, but Mum held her back.

Mum gave me a real row. You know the kind ...

WRONG TO TOUCH OTHER
PEOPLE'S THINGS
LOOK AT THE MESS YOU'VE MADE
GET IT CLEANED UP RIGHT NOW
PUT EVERYTHING BACK
THE WAY YOU FOUND IT

I wish Mum would tell that to Miranda when she messes with my toys. But she doesn't. Miranda gets off with everything. Just because she's older. It's not fair.

It took me ages to hoover up the talcum powder. The snow storm had got everywhere. Miranda stood over me with her arms folded.

And I hoovered up her best pink socks too. *Accidentally*, of course.

Well, the socks shouldn't have been lying under the bed. Mum's always telling us to put our things away, but I got sent to bed early anyway.

I was lying in bed thinking about Miranda and wondering what else I could do to annoy her when I suddenly thought of one GOOD thing about her. She's not afraid of spiders.

I am. Every time I go for a bath they always seem to pop up out of the plug hole. I think they come out to play the minute I take off my jersey. You can almost hear them saying:

Oh great, it's Benjamin's bath time. Let's have a run around and upset him. After you with the rubber duck, Incy.

Rubber duck coming up, Wincy.

That's when I yell for Miranda. She comes and chases them. Just shoos them back down the plug hole and puts the plug back in. She's really good with spiders in the bath.

If you really want a big sister, though, you can still have mine. I don't mind. I could give up having baths.

Maybe I shouldn't just give Miranda away for free, though. Maybe I should try to SWAP her first. I'd like to swap her for a puppy, but if I'm stuck with her, I'll ask for a puppy for Christmas.

THE
NEW PUPPY'S
TALE

The worst thing about being a puppy is, you never know what your new owner will be like.

I have two owners, Miranda and Benjamin. I was their Christmas present. You should have seen their faces when they first saw me on Christmas morning.

Miranda stood there staring at me, her eyes shining and her mouth wide open, while Benjamin jumped up and down, and couldn't stop grinning.

Then Miranda nearly hugged me to bits ...

... and Benjamin played chases with me round and round the Christmas tree, till we knocked the tree over and put out all the fairy lights. It was great!

Miranda and Benjamin had wanted a puppy for ages, but their mum had said, "Not until you're both old enough to look after it. A puppy is not just for Christmas. A puppy is for life."

Quite right too.

The next worst thing about being a puppy is, you never know what name your new owners will give you.

Miranda wanted to call me "Cuddles". Can you *believe* it? I know I'm very cuddly with my long floppy ears and spotty coat, but just think of what all the other dogs in the street would have said.

Red face time.

Benjamin wanted to call me "He-Man" even though I'm a dog. Can you imagine?

Ridiculous.

After a while they both agreed on Prince, but first they had to have ...
A PILLOW FIGHT.

AND A WATER FIGHT.

Then their mum appeared and gave them a real row. You know the kind ...

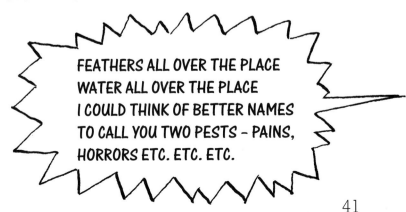

They were sent to bed early. I was glad. My floppy ears were sore listening to all their fighting. Brothers and sisters are very strange people. Why can't they be more like dogs?

The next time Miranda and Benjamin had a fight was in the pet shop.

"We'll buy Prince a lovely red tartan collar," said Miranda.

"No we won't. We'll buy him a thick brown leather one with big shiny studs."

"No we won't. Prince will look great in a red tartan one."

"Rubbish. He'll look great in a brown leather one with big shiny studs."

The owner of the pet shop listened to them fighting for a while, then he said, "Prince is only a little puppy, why not buy him a nice soft collar that won't hurt him while you're training him?"

It sounded like good sense to me, and they finally agreed to it.

The collar felt nice, and I looked very smart.

After that Miranda and Benjamin fought about who was to take me out walkies.

"Why don't you both take him?" sighed their mum.

Then they pulled the lead this way and that, and I was jerked about so much I felt my head was going to fall off.

That's when I gave my special bark. The one I keep for when I'm really cross. It starts way down deep in my tum, and works its way up till, instead of coming out in a little woof, it comes out in a great big

WURRRRF!

That stopped them fighting all right, and after that they took it in turns to take the lead.

Sometimes, though, Miranda and Benjamin don't fight. Sometimes they can be very nice; like on firework night, just after my first birthday.

There were lots of loud bangs that night when the fireworks went off, and I was shivering and feeling very frightened.

Miranda and Benjamin cuddled in on either side of me, and patted me, and stroked my head. That helped a lot, and I felt much better.

Then, another time, when I ran off into the woods, and got a thorn stuck in my paw, they carried me home. They took it in turns to bathe my paw and bandage it. That helped too, till they fought about which one of them had done most to make the paw better.

Really, why can't brothers and sisters be more like dogs and not fight with anyone?

Oh oh, wait a minute, I've just seen next door's cat sneak into MY garden. Where does she think SHE'S going? Who does she think SHE is? This is where *I* live. I must go and chase her.

Byeeeee.